Altars Built in Poetry
By Payton Golightly

1

contents

Author's Note
Part One - The Dark   4
"Scab" - a passage about trauma   49
Part Two - The Light   50
The Story of Him, The Story of Us   92

dedicated to The One who gave me the gift of words.

5

dear readers,

     You may be wondering, what does this book's title mean? Well, I will gladly explain!
     In Bible times, when someone went through a trial and God brought them out, they'd build an altar as a way of saying, "look what God did here." They'd make sacrifices to Him there to praise His name and each altar would remain as a marking for things God had done. It's commonly said that "altars have been built" throughout people's lives. Of course, we don't literally go build an altar out of stones, kill an animal, and burn it, but the altars today look different. For example, my altars are stamped all over different places and times in my life, but I think the biggest ones are found in my poetry! My writings are things I've built, (through God-given gifts) as I struggled, coped, and overcame every time I went through something. These are altars of my own which show what I've been through, where Christ has brought me now, and where He will bring me to in the future
     Each poem in this book has a story behind it, some of which I will tell to you in the following "Building the Altar" descriptions. "Building the Altar" stories will be testimonials about where the poem came from, what inspired it, and what God was doing or has done.
     A handful of my poems encounter tough topics that a few readers may be sensitive to. I ask that you please be careful in reading such poems. I would not want my poetry to trigger anything for you or cause you any form of difficulty. If you have been through

anything similar to these said poems, I apologize for the pain that has been on your heart, and I am proud of you for making it to where you are now. God has helped you to win every battle you have encountered so far, so keep going, keep fighting, seek and find healing in Him!

      My prayer and hope is that these words will help you get through hard times, as they did for me, that they will inspire you, and that they will bring you closer to The Lord. I pray that this book encourages you to look around at the altars built in your own life, see where Jesus has moved in your life, and be reminded that He has been The Provider and that He always will be!

The Dark

part one

"The Darkness"

Her demons visit her at night
They stay away when it's daylight
She tosses and turns as she attempts to sleep
They whisper about chains they hope she'll keep
They put up a really good fight
The darkness is her kryptonite

Her angels push the demons away
But it's pitiful because they're too late
She gave in then
But regrets it now
Her lips quiver, she lowers her brows
Tears begin to stream down
Regret, pain, and anger mixed into one
Thinking to herself, "WHAT HAVE YOU DONE?!"

Eye contact in the mirror
Look closer to see clearer
Million feelings in her eyes
Due to the pain of a reflection
That she no longer can recognize
A hundred questions
A thousand "why?!"'s

Curled up alone in the night
The darkness puts up a good fight
Sometimes she would just give in

12

Listening to lies told by devils with grins

The constant cycle of light and dark
Doubting she'll ever again find that joyful spark

"Communication issues"

"Communication is key"
You say
But the internet must be faulty
Or the carrier pigeon won't carry
Or the phone won't connect to my line
Or the messenger boy likes to tarry…

Or you're just like a parrot
Repeating words you heard
But don't understand

"Panic Attack"

Spiraling.
Darkness.
Confusion.
Fear.
"What is happening?"
"Why am I here?"

Anxiety rushing through her veins
"Who is even holding the reigns?"
Panic sinks in like a ship
Trying hard to get a grip
 A growing pain in her chest
Anxiety is an unwelcome guest

Panic attack
Everything looks white or black
"I just want the color back"
Loss of air
Burning lungs
Submerged in fire and water
The kind of feeling that seems like a slaughter
Tears blurring up her sight
Adding to the confusion she's trying to fight

Numbness spreading like a fire
"I can't keep doing this,
I'm just so tired"

Trying to breathe through the hiccups of tears
Been through so many of these over the years
Yet why can't she figure out how to get control?
"Why can't life be like taking a simple stroll?"

Panic attack
She wants her memory back
Everything is a blur
All their voices are a slur
Out of body
Out of mind
Feel like she's walking around blind

Curled up in the fetal position
Letting go of the "save me" mission
Quiet tears drip down her face
"Lord, take me from this horrid place"
Shaking and trembling
Her composed act is disassembling

Panic attack
"How much longer before I crack?"
Voice sad and high pitched
All control has been ditched
Finally giving in,
She sinks into the depths of anxiety's ocean

"Shower Thoughts"

Cry until my knees give out
Entering to panic attack stage
My tears come down in a fit of rage
That we're back here in this place

Curled up in the fetal position
Water running down my back
Tears running down my cheeks
As my poker face begins to crack
My hands go in my hair
As I tell myself to "stop"
Stop screaming
Stop yelling
Stop the fight inside
Stop the overthinking
Stop the never ending train
Of thoughts filled with anxiety
Stop the looping ride

Shower thoughts escaping
At every right turn
"Change the train of thought" I say
It loops around either way
I can't escape
And I can't outrun
These panicking motions
So I give into this train of thought

17

And let anxiety brew it's potions
Making me weaken
Making me fear
That I'm all alone
In here

When it's all over
I turn off the water
And step out of the curtain
Yes, I gave into that fight
But I'll beat the next, I'm certain

"Silent Tears"

Silent tears,
The most painful kind.
You put your hand over your mouth
To stifle a painful cry.
The worst pain?
The kind
You always have to hide.

"Colorless"

My life has lost its color
Its love
And its meaning
It's kind of strange
How I'm not even bleeding

Broken,
Hurt,
Insecure
No longer know what I'm looking for

Lost,
Hiding,
Constantly crying

Broken,
Beaten,
Completely defeated

What am I doing
How did I get here
Hardly even make it through the day
Without shedding a tear

Lost in this maze
Of confusion
And hurt
Where did this come from
Guess I took a wrong turn

Colorless

Joyless
Get me away from this

Help me
Save me
Fix me
Free me

My life lost its color
Its hope
And its feeling
It's almost crazy
That I'm still breathing

The lights went out
It all got dark
No love
Then no life
No loss,
I won't cry

But I did lose something
My color
To life
My meaning
My feeling

It walked right out
Never said a word
It lied
It ignored
Part of me died

But in the end there is no color
Just a broken heart
That's still somehow breathing
Even as it's bleeding

The color left a hole
That can not be fixed
It hurt me
It broke me
And now I'm learning

Never give away
Your happy heart
When you are unsure
From the very start
It's unhealthy
It's cruel
Driven by love's fuel

But it drained my color
 Losing my joy
To a stupid,
Immature,
But very valued boy

I loved him
I lost him
Along with all my color
I was naive enough to believe
That we could have lasted longer

Now the color is nearly gone
Even as I tried

To stand strong
For as long
As life let me survive
I feel like I'm fading
Losing love
Losing life,
Losing my mind

There is
Less color
I am colorless
As I fade into nothingness

"Breathe"

Inhale
Exhale
Pain in my lungs
"Breathe"
They say as anxiety
Overcomes

Inhale
Exhale
Racing heart
"Breathe"
They say as panic
Starts

Inhale
Exhale
Tingling fingers
"Breathe"
They say as leftover anxiety
Lingers

Inhale
Exhale
Peace after the storm
"You're breathing"
They say as I
Retake my calming form

"The Monster in the Attic"

Blank face
Outer space
Feeling her anxious heart race

Can't fight it
This silence
Like a wave crashing down
Flashbacks flashing all around

Loneliness
Broken bliss
She feels so stuffed in this

Little box
Big doll
Dress her up
Hair and all
Pushed inside
What a ride

Can't get it out of her head
Quiet screaming
Quiet crying
No fear of dying
Everything in silence
Has to stay just like this

Voice unheard
Memory blurred
TV static
Past's monster in the attic
It can't come down
Or your friend group will be a ghost town

Sad and scary
This monster's hairy
It has claws
Shark teeth like in the movie "Jaws"
Making her take a pause

Eyes like a slithery snake
How much more can the poor girl take?
Stuff it down
Snuff it out
This could give her the bad kinda clout

"Don't let them in, don't let them see
Be the good girl you always have to be"
This isn't the movie like Frozen
Your destiny isn't given it's chosen

Step out of the box
Break the attic door locks
Let out the monster inside
Vulnerable and broken
This'll be a bumpy ride

See all her scars?
See all her bruises?
Get in your cars
And drive away faster than cruise goes?

Yes she's been broken
Yes she's been hurt
Yes she's been used
Yes she's been bruised
Yes she's been thrown out
Yes she's been talked about
Yes ... she has an ugly past
Yes this monster's eyes look glassed

Yes she beat it
Yes she's won
Shot it down using her "Jesus" gun
Her monster's defeated
Even when it cheated

She's stronger than she was before
She and Jesus are knockin on Hell's door
Sayin, "'let my people go'
Sin is no winner, just the winner's foe!"
Truth reigns down
In the form of a thorn crown
To beat her monster to the ground

Shame has no power in His realm
Jesus' love did overwhelm
Monster out of the attic
Peace replacing the sound of TV static
Not ever alone in this
Full of Christ-given bliss
Winning this daily war
All because of the cross He willingly bore
To open up this once locked door

Blank face
Mind in outer space
Feeling her happy heart race
"Thank you for these blessed days"

No more deafening silence
No more fear
The monster from the attic
Is no longer here

Building the Altar:

Although this poem is not exactly one that fits perfectly in the "Dark" part of this book, there is a darkness in the way it begins. Oftentimes when those who are believers have struggles, a past, a trial, or any sin this thing called "shame" begins to fester. Shame is not for us, nor is it from God. We find ourselves trying to fit within the box of impossible standards in order to please people, especially those in the church. We don't want them to know our darkness and our secrets because we are so afraid of the unknown that we wish the unknown to be our habitat. The truth is that every testimony is important and every story which holds the name of Jesus has power. So why hide? Share what He has done because the truth is that anything He has/had His hands on can be used for His glory and our good! Don't let the monster control you!

"Just say no"

"Just say no" they'll whisper in your ear
But they don't understand that's hard to do
And it's easier to hear
"Just say you don't want to
It's really not hard"
But when he's manipulative
And you are naïve
He can quickly sway you like the wind on a leaf
When he touches you places you don't want him to
You can't say no because here's what he'll do
He'll make up excuses to make it okay
He says he'll be "happier this way"
He gets you all flustered and takes his chance
You can't move with the surprise
When his hands go in your pants
You want to say no and to push him away
But you know he won't allow it
You know what he'll say
He'll say that he promised he'd do that one day
But you had tried to say no and he did it anyway
He kisses you places you don't want him to
You hate every moment
He pretends he doesn't have a clue
"Just say no" everyone would say
But what'd you do if you end up in that position one day?

"Lips Like Poison"

Your lips on my lips were like poison
Your hands on my body left stains
The color of all my feelings
Were the bruises that showed for my pain

"It's Not the Same"

You lust instead of love
And say that it's the same
But ice feels different
Than a burning, scorching flame

Building the Altar:

I never knew what lust really was until I experienced it. I was once told by a young man that he was "in love" with my body. In the moment, I was naïve and inexperienced in all things involving emotions as deep as love so I didn't yet recognize the flags of deep red waving in my face. I didn't end the relationship there, looking back, I so wish I had. I am here to tell any young woman that love and lust are far different from one another. Please look out for and recognize the signs because I guarantee they will be there if he is not the man meant for you. Pray. That is the best advice I can give you. Prayer is more powerful than anything I could tell you to do. Pray for your future spouse, pray for your current relationship status, (single or not) that it would be Christ-centered, and pray for any relationship, or even friendship, that you may be considering getting into. The truth is that no one can be more discerning of those things than He, so look to Him and listen to Him. Obey what He decides because, as one of my friends likes to say to herself, sometimes "rejection is God's protection". Don't be controlled by the wrong things or for the wrong feelings because it will only leave you hurting. Walk in obedience, in step with what He has in store for you and know that He always knows best.

"Doormat"

I sit around and wait for you
To walk all over me
Our friendship is a one-way street
And I'm only here for you to wipe your feet

You don't care where I'm at
Until you need a doormat
I'm sick and tired of sitting here
I definitely wasted every tear

I'm done being your doormat
You can't even deny that
You only come to me for your convenience
Can't believe I gave you so much lenience

I'm not doing this anymore
Don't know what I did all that for
My bleeding heart for hurting people
Sent me rolling down this steep hill

Wrapped around your finger
I let those feelings linger
And now I regret every word
Every good memory is slowly being blurred

I'm tired of being your doormat
I'm not gonna wait until you wanna "chat"

I'm not gonna stay here for you to wipe your feet
I don't do friendships that will only leave me beat

You drained all my energy
My happiness came down with tears
I sacrificed myself trying to make you happy
Lost myself, creating my biggest fears

My Nana told me, "no more!",
"What are you doing all this for?
He's not worth all your pain
And I can see that this is plain:
He's not the person that you want or need
Let someone else water that seed!"

Earlier I saw an Instagram post
Saying, "don't settle for less, only for most"
Another said, "Stop trying to be friends with
People who want you one day
But don't even see you the next."
Nana told me to "leave him" in a long text

"He's not worth losing your joy,
Don't give that power to a *stupid* teenage boy!
Smile and laugh and just be you!
Then you can see what he will do:
He'll regret that he left.
He'll feel sorry for moving on.

You're worth far more than how he treated you all along!
You're not in *his* game, he is *your* pawn."

I'm done being your doormat
I won't be friends with a brat
I'm not here for your convenience
I'm no longer giving you lenience

I won't sit around and wait for you
To walk all over me
I'm sick and tired of waiting here
I will never waste another tear

"The Cost"

My goal was to make you happy
At any and every cost
I didn't realize that price
Would be *myself* getting lost

"Trauma Talk"

We talk about our feelings.
We talk about our health.
Depression, anxiety, pain.
We talk about suicide.
We talk about how to deal with such things,
But trauma can't be the same?

"Keep it quiet,
Keep it silent.
We don't wanna know.
Suffer in silence.
That struggle is your own.
Cover it up,
Shut it up,
We don't want it shown."

Why can't we speak of trauma?
Why is that so wrong?
Are you scared to know of the darkness?
Scared of the world's true song?
Are you nervous to be called out?
Does the truth make you squirm?
Even more the reason for me to speak out
Even more the reason for me to be firm

I'll tell them about my trauma.
I'll tell them what I know.
And even if they don't wanna,

I'll make them hear of every woe.
I will not sit in silence.
I will not be a "good girl".
I won't listen to you for once.
My trauma will be spoken,
My story will be shown.

I'll talk about my feeling.
I'll talk about my health.
But I can't speak of these things
Without speaking of that trauma
With which I've dealt.

"Memories"

She smiled with tears rolling down her face.
A flash of a thousand memories and thoughts of someone she couldn't replace.
"I'm glad you're happier now", she said, her voice barely a whisper.
Her blue eyes were a sea of tears,
A window to her heart, broken in pieces,
But he never noticed because he wasn't looking at hers.

She remembered a million memories of him, the good things.
Inside jokes and laughter.
Smiles full of joy. Joy he brings.
The look in his eyes when he stared into hers,
The feeling of his arms wrapped tightly around her,
The smell of his hoodie,
The sound of his laughter,
The sight of his smile,
She never thought their relationship could turn vile.
So many things racing through her mind
As she stood before him, broken inside.

So many promises broken and memories ruined...
No longer happy but full of confusion...

"Did he mean when he said this? was he lying to me?"
So many thoughts of doubt and anxiety....

Once she told him that some of the worst pain is when
Someone you talk to everyday goes silent or leaves you....
She told him one of her biggest fears was that she had him to lose....
He said he agreed, he could never lose her....
And yet, he moved on like none of those memories or feelings had ever occurred.

Tears running down her cheeks,
She watches as the weeks
Drag him further from her.
Invisible and nonexistent.... alone in the pain.
"He's smiling now, shouldn't I do the same?
Why does it hurt so much?! Why can't I move on?!
Why is he so happy when all those memories are gone?!!"

So many thoughts of anxiety,
Doubt and confusion.... "he must have lied to me"
"Does he ever even think of me now?
If not then I want to ask, how?!"

The pain never stops
And the flashbacks hurt

"Why do I have to be such a flirt?!"
Never thought things would get to where they were
Never thought he would really hurt her

Too many memories
Too many pictures
"Why do I get so attached so easily?!
I'm either really stupid or very silly!"

Walls go back up and good memories become painful
Trust issues and depression
Self hate and anxiety
"SOMEONE PLEASE COME SET ME FREE!!!"
Nights begging out for Jesus to take her away
Nights and nights she'll hope, cry, and pray
"No one wants me or needs me, why am I here?!"
So much pain, laced with fear

"Lord take me home!
What is the point?!"
Feels like she's drowning
"There's too much noise!!"

Day after day
Week after week
Feels like all she can do is sink
And if only she could get some sleep!!

Go through the motions

Fake all the smiles
"No one can know that you go through trials"
Everyone's worried
And trying to fix her
Sending her songs and verse after verse
All she has is the flashbacks and replays
She wishes to go back to the good ol' days

She walks around, secretly pained
All of this acting leaves her drained
No one knows what she's going through
No one could understand...
Before him life was completely grand
Now all she feels is depression and self hate
When she thinks of him her eyes dilate
And now she can say that these sad songs relate

All the voices in her head telling her what to do
Gosh, she just wishes she could stay home from school
"Put on the fake face
Pretend you're okay!
Push through and
Use lemons to make
Lemonade!"
"But how's that worked out so far for me?!
I don't feel happy
And I don't feel pretty!!"

And when everything goes silent

And she can't hear a word
Anxiety creeps in and demands to be heard
All these voices whispering in her head
"Would they even miss you if you were dead?"
A thousand flashbacks and memories
Thoughts of someone she can't replace
If only he saw the pain written on her face

"I'm done with this cycle
I'm done with this pain
Nothing is changing, you just stay the same.
I'm letting you go now,
Making us both a vow
I'm not gonna sacrifice myself to try to be your friend
And so, goodbye. This is finally the end."

She smiles with tears rolling down her face.
A flash of so many memories she wishes she could erase.

"Thoughts I Get Because of You"

I found myself thinking,
"Prepare yourself to lose them,"
The first day I was with him.
"They all leave,
They always do,"
I thought as I readied myself
To lose him.

I found myself detaching
Before I ever got attached.
Because if I was stuck to him,
I'd struggle more once he
Was gone.

I found myself painless
When he really walked away.
I cried because I didn't feel like crying.
I cried because I had pushed feelings away.
I cried because I'd prepared myself
So well for losing him
That when I did
I had already rid
The sadness of our unglue.

I find myself now thinking
Any time I start to get attached,
"Prepare yourself to lose them.

Their feelings and friendship won't last."

I find myself struggling to trust, again
Because if I do
I might just get hurt
By someone I called a friend.

And so, sitting here,
I find myself thinking,
"They'll leave you too."
But all I wanna do
Is trust that they aren't like
Everyone else…

Everyone else.
And you.

"Past"

I thought you'd be in my future
But instead you'll stay in my past
At least I have memories that will forever last

"New Character"

Introducing a new character,
He walks on the stage.
This is the next act.
A script's turned page.

Introducing a new character
What will he be?
A cause for grief?
A comedic relief?
A comfort
Or a pain?
Will he be entertaining
Or simply lame?

The audience sits in silence
What will he be?
I wonder what this act will look like
What's the new theme for me?

"Watching From The Outside"

You're viewing my Instagram stories
Instead of being in them.
You're watching me live my life
Instead of being in it.
You see me dancing to my song,
Knowing you will never again dance along.
What's it like to watch from the outside
And miss being in?

You used to be in it all,
But now
You've only been
Viewing my stories,
And watching me dance.
Missing the life on the inside
As you watch from the out.

"A Fork In The Road"

Her kindred spirit that was lost
As he ran the marathon to Death
Refusing the Love from the cross
Refusing the renewing Breath
Because of his constant want for more
Because of his constant hunger
Path split with a fork in the road
One chose destruction
One chose Hope
A path of Joy, a path of Life
A path of pain, a path of strife
Loneliness and brokenness
Versus Fellowship and Wholeness
A friend's heart breaks for another
As she watches him stumble and wander

"Butterflies in My Stomach"

My stomach used to do flips and turns
When I was around you
Flips of joy and turns of happiness
But now, hurt is all those turns do
My stomach has spun so much
That now it's just a knot
And now that we've expired
My stomach just hurts a lot

The butterflies that used to get excited around you
Still spin and flutter all about
But now it's with anxiety
Threatening to come up and out
Instead of hopes and daydreams
Instead of dancing to sweet tunes
They flutter in a painful craze
Every time that my eyes meet your gaze

"The Game of Heartbreak"

Heartbreak is my least favorite game
And yet I seem to keep on playing
Everytime a relationship seems to be going good
It ends faster than I think it should
Over and over, this game I play
Hoping it'll cease to say
"Game over" on the screen display
Big, fat, red letters across the screen
Ugh, Heartbreak just has to make a scene
But after every fit of pain
I turn the computer back on
And play it again

"It's Better This Way"

Just wanted to make you happy
Or make you less lonely
Regrets are all I'm left with
Don't think you'll ever say or be sorry
And sometimes I wish we ended as friends,
Not enemies, but I know it's better this way

"You"

I wish I could stop writing poetry about you
But writing is the only thing I can seem to do
It spins in my head
When I'm trying to go to bed
It always comes up at the most inconvenient times
Like when I'm in the shower, in class,
Or when I'm trying to drive

My thoughts compile into a stanza
That turns into a story
And the main character is always you

In times of anger
In times of pain
In times where I wish to escape my brain
Poetry comes out smoothly
Like a flying plane
I wish I didn't see you
In everything

"Regrets"

My life is filled with plenty of regrets
One of those is you
I regret a few things I said
But at least all I said to you was true
I know you can't say the same
There's too many lies for me to name

"Copy & Paste"

Oh, I'll find another boy like you.
Boys like you are simply everywhere.
You're like a copy and paste,

but you'll never find another girl like me.
Women like me are few and rare.
And for us, life is so unfair
for all the time we waste
On boys who're like a copy and paste.

Building the Altar:

Yes, this poem was written in a very angry moment of mine. And maybe I can admit that it was a little dramatic, but I will never say that it was unfair or untrue. There are many *boys* who are exactly alike, predictable and generic. The truth is that when women settle for less than a man, a *boy* is what they end up with. They can be found easily because they are everywhere and anywhere. They give less than the bare minimum and more often than not, their heart is not in the right place, especially not for them to be in a relationship with someone like you! If you take anything away from this poem, take this: Don't settle for less. Ever. You're worth so much more than that.

"I Don't Miss You Anymore"

I don't miss you anymore.
I thought I always would before.
But the truth is I don't feel anything
For you.
And I don't miss you anymore.

You didn't leave a hole
That was too big to fill.
I thought you would and that
I'd miss you still.
But the truth is...
You didn't leave that large a gap,
And I don't need a map
To get back
To where I was before
You.

I don't miss you anymore.
Life is more colorful,
Where I thought it'd be blue...
And honestly?
I don't miss you.

"Do I Scare You?"

You hold me with two fingers,
An arms-length away.
Like a bug or dirty clothing item
You want to throw away.
Like something dangerous,
Gross,
Or scary.
You're tempted to run.
But I'm just a heartbroken girl,
Wishing for her friend.
Although I guess we both have wounds
That will take time to mend.

"The Night You Tried to Commit"

Everything was still moving.
Everyone was still going.
But time for me had stopped.
Everything but instinct shut down
When I read that text and my heart dropped.
I can't live this life without
You in the same proximity.
I'm so afraid if it was my fault
Did this have anything to do with me?
"I really don't want you to leave",
I thought as I stood outside your front door
BANG! BANG! BANG!
I slammed my fist into it and yelled your name.
Trembling I fumbled for my phone,
"Mom, she's not answering the door"
Next thing I know we're back in the car.
Headed for the emergency room,
There was a voice in my brain,
Telling me you would be staying.
But emotion drowns out logic
As fear takes over my body.
Tears begin to come but I won't let them roll.
We're in the emergency room, next thing I know.
"She's gonna be okay," they said,
"They have charcoal in her system."
I'm still terrified but I believe them.
You're gonna be okay.

You'll be fully healed one day.
And until then I will faithfully pray.

Building the Altar:

I won't tell you this story further than I have, but I just want to say a few things.

Mental health awareness is so important. I have seen numerous friends grow to be overcome with the struggles of different mental health issues over the years. Anxiety, depression, suicidal thoughts, tendancies, and attempts have all been heartbreakingly common in the lives of those around me. I just wish to say that my heart and prayers go out to you who battle mental health, love someone who is fighting, have loved one who was lost to the fight, or have experienced any form of the affects of mental health struggles. You are deeply loved and cared for. Though the darkness seems to be overwhelming, there is a Light that shines brighter than the darkness could ever imagine. These things are not what

God meant for us when He created the world. His heart breaks for the brokenness of sin in His creation.

  If you or someone you know are experiencing any form of suicidal thoughts, tendancies, or ideas, please contact someone. Family members, teachers, friends, hotlines, anything or anyone to get help. Just please do not try to hide and fight this on your own. Though you may feel alone, you certainly are not, there are people who want to help you or get you help. Please let someone know what you are dealing with. Just like you need to take care of a broken bone for it to heal, you must take care of your mental health in order to get better. Don't let it go untreated.

  You are loved by the One who is called Love. As much as you feel to be fighting this battle alone, He will always be fighting by your side.

"Pretty Ugly Weeds"

Everybody knows the truth about weeds
And what they do to blooming seeds.
They choke them out and steal their food.
Creating an environment where they can't breathe,
They take down the weak
In a competition for sunlight and a drink.
No room to share
Because they believe they're
The better of the two.
But we all know what is really true,
Weeds aren't any better than seeds,
Simply devils disguised as plants
And liars that try to justify why they're tyrants.

Everybody knows the truth about those ugly weeds
But sometimes there are people who fail to see
There's more than one who wishes to destroy the seeds.
Some weeds are simple and easy to find
But to the others, some are blind.
There's another kind that creep on through:
The ones that have manipulative blooms.
They look real pretty while they choke good seeds out

With a fake smile on, they cause a seedling's drought.
No sun, no rain, just a trap with this pretty weed.
Alone is this poor, dying seed.
People pass and think, "what a pretty flower",
But they don't know the evil truth of what it's after.
They don't see it's intents
Hidden in the pretty petals' glints.

So what's the difference between these two weeds?
Nothing, except the way they choke the seeds.
One is obvious and the other masked,
But they both destroy the good for the bad.
Pretty weeds and ugly weeds,
They're the same on the inside.
One is just more confident,
Manipulative, and shiney enough it doesn't feel
The need to hide

So now you know the truth about both these horrid weeds.
Now the question is if you'll take action
Or let them destroy your seeds.

"Scab" - a passage about trauma - by one of my closest friends, Jade

isn't it crazy how trauma works. one day you think you're fine and the next it floods back into your head. sometimes you sleep like it never even happened and yet there are nights where it feels like that's the only thing that can ever cross my mind. we obviously weren't so different because we were close at one point, best friends i thought at one time, but i think the one difference between you and me however is that it never crossed your mind at all. you were not phased by the way you treated me because you justify your actions under the false pretense that you are a good person. you make me out to be stupid, like i "don't know what im talking about". your friends justify being friends with you because it "never happened to them". but my situation is not one in its own because you've done this to not just me, but two other girls. two other individuals with the same story as me. righteous anger is real and powerful, but i'm tired of picking at a scab when all it does is bleed. if you pick a scab it will never heal so here in this moment i choose to forgive you so that I can heal.

The Light
part two

"The Tunnel"

This tunnel seems to go forever
But there's an end where I see a light
It may be dark right now
But what I see at the end
Shines incredibly bright

This tunnel won't last forever
One day I'll emerge on the other side…
But right now I feel stuck…
I know He'll dry the tears I've cried…
But right now I feel stuck in a muck,
A tunnel that's cramped and dark.
The only hope is the spark
Of light at the end
Where I get to spend
Eternity in joy in Him

"The Light"

The sun comes up
It's a new day
The Light always comes
And pushes the darkness away

"Daughter of The King"

Medium boobs
Skinny waist
Pretty face
Soft skin
But he didn't see the true beauty that was within

He said that he loved her
But it must have come out wrong
He said he loved her body
Wasn't her personality also strong?

He fell for her looks
And only that
Said she was good enough
But that lie was big and fat
It was too easy for him to forget ever saying that

Abandoned, she felt broken
Alone and confused
Was she not enough?
Had she been used?
So many questions ran through her head
It took her so long to forget what he'd said

Months went by as she grew and grew
Learning new things she never knew
She forgave and moved on

Learning her testimony was strong

Gathering her thoughts
She wrote him a letter
Thinking it would make her feel better
But closure wouldn't come 'til the letter was delivered
Fearful tears welled up and her lip quivered
She prayed to the Lord saying
"Help this to go only as You will it"

It was a Friday morning
When she faced her fears
Her friends behind her with prayers and cheers
She told him all of the truth
And oh, that closure felt so good!
She knew it could hurt him
But if only he understood

The pain that he put her through
The long tearful nights
Times where she had to put up mental fights
Demons banging on every door
She once wondered what she was here for

Shame and weakness pressed her down
But Jesus wouldn't let her fall flat on the ground
He lifted her up, forgiving her sin
Making her stronger

From the outside and in
"His power is made perfect
In our weaknesses."
She now knows that she is His

Daughter of The King!
Wearer of a crown!
She has True power when those demons come around
Stronger than she's ever been
True joy from the Father
Joy, she could never find in another

Codependency beat by "royalty"
Anxiety beat by "trustworthy"
Self-hate beat by "I'm enough"
Jesus gives you more than just the "good stuff"

She learned to forgive
But never forget
It's the mistakes that shape you
When you find solace in Him
She learned to love
From afar
To pray for your persecutors,
For the people who break your heart,
And for the people the leave the deepest of scars

Scars show us where we've been

And where we now are
A testimony of how Christ heals
And brings us farther than far

Freed from the constant weight of guilt
She's like a beautiful flower that won't wilt
Her confidence is found in the Lord above
Her heart overflows with His abundant love
Peace like a river
And joy like a flood
She is washed clean in the Savior's blood
A new identity in the King
She is given a reason to sing
A crown on her head
And the Lord in her heart
She wears a new title as her next chapter starts

"Glue"

You glue me together,
Piece by piece,
But I miss my old form.
You stick the shattered pieces together
And somehow this mess
Becomes Your art.

I am an abstract of broken pieces,
But they're beautiful together.
I may not look the same as I used to
But at the same time,
I now look better.

Building the Altar:

Imagine someone breaks a beautiful vase on the floor. The shattering sound is heartbreaking to the artist, but in the broken mess, he sees an opportunity for an even more beautiful creation. He gathers the pieces together and glues them together with the hands of a master. When the vase is repaired, he steps back in awe, admiring the abstract art even more beautiful than the original piece. This is the picture and the story that was born from a time of hurt and pain that I was experiencing. In the process of coping with my overwhelming emotions and my heartbreak, Jesus stooped down and spoke to me in the words I understand most, poetry. These emotions of pain, sorrow, and mourning can become so beautiful in the eyes of the One who created us. When we break, He is the One who glues us back together! Though He may not remove our scars in the process, He creates something of *new* beauty!

"It's Okay"

Sunrise and sunset
The beauty of the sky
Clouds of rain
Or clouds of snow
Or others just for shade
This makes me be in awe of all that You have made
The wind blowing through the leaves
In the tall, beautiful trees
And in the breeze
I hear You say
"Everything, will be okay"

"Raise My Hands"

I raise my hand
In worship and begin to think…
I never understood
How one could stand
During worship
And never, ever move.
I don't think I ever will
Wrap my mind around the idea
Of being completely still
As the band plays
In complete praise
For the One who saved us all.
The lyrics are a melody
That can't measure up to who You are,
And yet there they stand
Without lifting a hand
To You.
And maybe anxiety is the reason?
Maybe they feel held back?
Is it the publicity of it all?
Maybe they're under spiritual attack?
Whatever boundary,
And whatever wall,
I'm glad I made it here
Because no matter the judgment,
No matter the fear,
My hands and voice will be lifted

To joyfully cheer.
Because You deserve the glory.
You deserve the praise.
You deserve more than a song
And a small hand raised.
I want to scream Your name from mountains,
And speak it over my life.
I want to speak it over my friends,
My family,
Every circumstance and strife.
You're name is like no other!
There's not one that could compare!
Because we were sinners against You
And yet You took those sins to bear!
We placed a crown of thorns upon You,
Yelled jeers, cursed Your name.
We beat and mocked and killed You,
Yet for us You took the blame.
We no longer hold the weight
Of the guilt, of the shame.
And for that, You have many names
You are Great.
You are Good.
You are King of Kings.
You turned these rags to riches
And make the impoverished royalty.
You are Messiah,
Son of God,
The One who came to save,

You are the resurrected One,
Who defeated sin, and death, and grave.
You are Love
To those who need it
And to those who feel unworthy.
And for all these things
I have reason to praise.
You deserve all the glory!
So I'll raise my hands in worship,
And I'll sway, jump, and sing,
Because if You are so good to a sinner like me,
Then I will surely give You everything!

"Sometimes"

Sometimes you have to wander
And wonder
Before you can discover
Sometimes you must get lost
Before you can be found
Sometimes we swim
Until we've almost drowned
Sometimes you have to journey
To get to the dream destination
And thirst before
Finding hydration
And sometimes you have to ride a roller coaster
Before you can stop and get off into peace
And sometimes it takes pain
To create the most out of the least

"Firefly Light"

Fall in love on a summer night
Staring at Your creation in the firefly light
Sunset blazing
Star gazing
Thankful for the beauty of it all
Blessed in the Joy of firefly light
You shine on my world even in the night
And I'm so grateful to You
Because the things You speak
Always become true
And I will always be
In awe that I have
A God who loves me
Like you do

"In His Eyes"

They say "thick thighs"
"Skinny waist"
"Big butt"

They say
"She needs to be nice
But no soft girls for me
She can't wear makeup
But she has to be pretty
She should wear something hot
But not too revealing
She should have curly hair
But it shouldn't be frizzy"

But some of us don't have that
They put us in a box
And pick us to pieces
It's so hard to think
To think, or to breath in
How can I live
When you tell me to be perfect
How can I be my best
When you say my best isn't worth it

The constant pain
The constant crying
Some girls... even think of dying

Days of starvation
Don't say a word
"Don't tell us the complications"
They don't want us to be heard

Social media tells me how to look
With ads about diets
And new ways to cook
Commercials that tell me how to lose weight
If I do any more, I might waist away
Look in the mirror
I only see her
The girl who is insanely insecure

They tell us "work harder"
"Work more"
Then, "Work less"
"Cook in the kitchen!"
And "Clean up this mess!"

What happened to the love from fairy tales?
The happily ever after?
The colorful ending?
But sadly, that's no longer trending

Small nose
Almond eyes
Symmetrical face
Some of us only have the skinny waist

Stop picking me apart
Don't tell me who to be
I'm beautiful in His eyes
He's the only one I need

He doesn't care about the outside
He cares about my heart
He tells me He cares for me
He heals all my scars
He wraps me in mercy
Something I do not deserve
He loves all my bruises
My scratches
My scars
He says "You're perfect
Just the way you are"

All the boys of this world,
All the fairy tale endings
Can't compare to my God
And the love I'm now feeling

Don't let them tell you to change
Don't listen to the lies
You're beautifully made
And perfect in His eyes
He knit you together
And called you good

So you should know
He never lies when He calls you
Beautiful

"Keep on moving"

The earth is still turning
And the sun is still shining
The moon is still bright
And the stars still fill
The darkness of night
But your spot in my life is now empty
I'm left alone with the happy memories
But life keeps on moving
And time keeps on passing
And I cherish these memories that are forever lasting
I have no regrets and I have no fears
Because I know that my God is still here
I don't need a boyfriend...
Though I wish I had my best friend
But I understand you need time
And that maybe this friendship will end
It's okay if you don't want me
And I completely understand
But none of these memories will haunt me
And I'm glad that for a while I could hold your hand
So thank you for the memories and thank you for the good stories
Thank you for making me feel safe instead of sorry
Of course it still hurts

And of course there is pain
But I have to take the next logical steps
Towards growing flowers in the garden
Where it seems to constantly rain

"Single"

Most say that singleness is sad
But I think that it's pretty rad
Because if I was focused on someone else
I would be unable to focus on myself
And often we need a single phase in order to
learn to first give Him praise
Single doesn't mean alone
It just means you're in a growing zone
Singleness is so often misunderstood
When it should be seen as something good
People seem to always make a fuss
But singleness is often
The very best when
We search for and find the best version of us
So for those of you in a single phase
Try not so hard to rush
Because you'll miss the lesson in the craze
Of you chasing after the next crush

"Overflow"

When they're the right person,
I promise you'll know
Because you'll both be seeking the things you should
And those things will simply make you glow
When your love for Jesus begins to show
That is when you
Go from one,
To a perfect pair of two
Because in that moment he will know
He's fallen in love with the overflow

"Seasons"

January.

The freezing cold.
A new beginning
To replace the old.

February.

A period
Of love
Or heartbreak.
The real permanence
Or the heartache.
Red and pink
The color theme linked
With this one of love
or brokenness.

March.

A transition
From cold to rain,
With the possibility of snow.
This is a weird one
Many forget to know
As the beginning of spring.
The end of the darkness

Replaces by beautiful new things.

April.

Rain and
Flowers,
Growth
from warm showers.
The rising after the setting
A favorite none are caught forgetting.

May.

The beginning of warmth
With continued rains.
Colors all over nature
And joy in the air.
This one is so beautiful,
It's almost unfair.

June.

Summer sun
And rampant fun.
Loads of memories
For everyone!

July.

Bright days
With the sun at full blaze.
Joy, sweat, smiles, and laughter.
Left with a good tan after.
Lots of photos
And videos
To capture snippets of the good times
As life just goes and goes.

August.

The end and the beginning.
Goodbye summer!
Hello school!
This has the best two pieces
And is pretty cool.
As the heat increases
You get to take homework breaks
In the swimming pool.

September.

The heat begins to drop
Summer officially comes to a stop.
And you're deeper into the year.
Fall is just around the corner
And the decorations start to appear.

October.

Spooky season has arrived.
No one is pumpkin spice deprived.
Cooler weather,
Colored leaves,
There is beauty in fall's trees.

November.

Thankfulness
And the complete fall bliss.
Family,
Fires,
Big meals,
And crazy Black Friday buyers.

December.

The biggest holiday of the year,
Christmas time,
Where everyone is full of cheer.
Warm treats
And drinks
In cold weather.
Heaters to make us feel better.
Blankets by a cozy fire
With the radio playing christmas choir.
The end of another blessed year
Excitement for the one that is almost here.

"Fields"

A field of grass
Spreads before me
Swaying in the winds that pass
Peace engulfing every part
Of my heart made out of glass
Spinning 'round with eyes shut tight
It's a cloudy day with the perfect amount of sunlight
The sound of rustling under my feet
The scent of the earth in my lungs, so sweet
Swaying with the wind and grass
Praying this is a feeling to always last

"Sweet"

Summer is one of my favorite seasons
And there are about a million reasons
Smoothies with friends
Hoping this never ends
Burn, peel then tan
Long drives in a van
Summer dresses
"Summer love"
Singing praises to God above
Camps for weeks
Teens' joy at their peaks
Strawberries
Blueberries
Spitting out seeds of cherries
Ice cream cone
So many colors shown
Reading books
Giving friends funny looks
Cookies and candy
My hair is all sandy
Beach baby
Peach baby
Watermelon and sweets maybe?
Dancing in the rain
Healing from past pain
Sunset vibes
Starry nights

Warmth and heat
Cheeks colored pink
Polaroids and picture frames
Let go of school's chains
Bible studies
Hang out with buddies
Eat tons of chips
Go on mission trips
Wear long ugly shorts
And so many t-shirts
Ultimate frisbee and volleyball
Too bad I'm not athletic at all
New friends, old friends
Getting to know friends
Fake friendship ends
Windows rolled down
As you drive around town
Scream to music in the car
Taking trips, don't go too far
Thrift shopping
Popcorn popping
Saturday and Sunday
Go back to work on Monday
Firepit and s'mores nights
Fireflies are our lights
Stargazing
All of nature seems to be praising
Burgers and fries
Swatting away flies

Play with the dog
The boys will probably catch a frog
Yellow, green, and light blue
Remember all the good things are true
Spending time on a boat
Falling asleep on a pool float
Butterflies and sleepless nights
Going over wrongs and rights
Sand and seashells
Share secrets no one ever tells
Outdoor movie
Acting goofy
Eat mangos and pineapples
Acting like the biggest fools
The teens might need some therapy
Maybe do some painting
Late night crying
Homemade donuts frying
Sit by a crackling fire
Talking to friends 'til you tire
Dancing in the shower
Sweat stained shirts
Meeting cute flirts
Splash around in a creek
Only motivated to work out for one week
Popsicles
Swimsuits and pools
Cute new hair
Get everyone to stare

Coffee or tea
Toes in the waves of the sea
Relax after work
Summer is the best perk
Saltwater
Freshwater
It just keeps getting hotter
Photographs
Giddy laughs
Smiles and grins
Fishies with fins
The smell of flowers and mown grass
So glad we're out of class
Go on walks
Late-night talks
Spend a day by the lake
How many marshmallows can you take
Little plants in the window sill
Sit outside while your dad starts to grill
Clouds with rain they'll begin to fill
White clouds
Gray clouds
Fluffy and chunky clouds
Dancing and singing
Ignore that my phone is ringing
Hair flying in the breeze
Love the look of green trees
Long texts and facetimes
Everyone in their primes

Sun on my face
Oh! How I love this place!
I wish summer were endless
I could continue to live like this

"The Tallest Tree"

Little seed in the ground,
Beautiful trees all around.
"When will I get tall like them?!
I'm not even as tall as that little stem!
I'm the size of a crumb!!"
The little seed looked sad and glum,
Thinking that he looked dumb.

Little sprout in the ground,
He's taller now, but he still feels down.
"When will I be a big tree?!
All my friends are taller than me!"
The poor little sprout.
All he could do was pout.

Little twig in the ground,
Barely weighing 2 whole pounds.
"I'm getting there!! You'll all see!!
I'm gonna be a big big tree!!"
The little twig, he tried so hard,
To become the biggest tree in the yard.
He worked and he ate,
Knowing that one day he could be great

Big tree in the ground,
He's taller than any other tree around.
All that work payed off.

The other trees had said he couldn't do it with a scoff.
"I'm tall now! I knew I could do it!
And everyone said I should quit!"
The happy tree lived out his days,
Warm and joyful in the sun's rays.

The tallest tree in the ground
Cheering on the seeds he sees around
"When will we get tall like you?"
"Once you decide you really want to.
And I know it's something you can do!"

Building the Altar:

Make of this what you will, but my heart behind this poem may not be exactly what most would expect. Oftentimes, we try to strive towards material or superficial goals in life. Some people wish the goal would come but do nothing to reach it, others work to get there, and some beat themselves up in their strive to become "the best". In my life, the most important goal is that of Spiritual growth. I have been through each of the phases and landed in the middle. First, doing nothing but wishing for a stronger relationship with God. Second, beating myself up over never doing enough, no matter what I did. Now, I simply put in the work. I learned that it's not about the quantity of time spent in God's Word, but about the quality of it. If I read 4 chapters of Scripture in one morning and understand nothing, it would mean nothing in comparison to the morning I spend just striving to fully understand 1 verse. Growing in the faith is all about consistency and quality in time with God. Set your mind to achieving your goals and know that the voices that say you can't are not of God or for you.

"Legos"

My childhood was built
In blocks of every color.
Red and blue
And green and purple
And all things in between.
Those blocks were my every day
And my everything.
Build and take apart,
My first acts of true art.
Independent and creative,
My every gift request
From every relative.
"I want this one."
Then another.
Our floor was simply covered.
Hours, I would spend,
Sitting in my little town.
Colors and creativity were all around,
Fueling the fire
That was my young mind.
I wish every childhood was built like mine.

"Birds in flight"

Soaring high above the sky
Like birds that can fly
Spinning,
Twisting,
Turning,
Swaying,
Two birds singing and playing

From the nest
To the highest height
Beautiful birds in graceful flight
Enjoying the warm sunlight

They fell first in order to fly
Fell so far they thought they'd die
And then they lifted into the sky
Joyful tweets
Soft wing beats
Pretty song
They both sing along

And then as they tire
They perch on a wire
Side by side
They'll sleep through the night
And tomorrow they'll take on a new height

"Flowers"

Flowers are a door
To my heart
To my soul
Give me flowers
And I'll love you
'Til the day we grow old

"What's Your Favorite Color?"

"What's your favorite color?",
Asks one of her friends.
"I'm not so sure,"
She replies as she grins.

"I've always loved blue.
The color of the sky.
The oceans
And seas.
The color of my eyes
And of yummy berries."

"So is blue your favorite color?"
Her friend proceeds to ask.
"Well, I'm not so sure,"
She says as she laughs.

"I've always loved yellow.
The color of the sun.
The color of lemons,
Bright sunflowers, birds,
And bumblebees.
Of the daffodils that brighten fields."

"So is yellow your favorite color?"
The friend asks with a giggle.
"Well, I'm not so sure"
She says with a smile
That makes her nose wriggle.

"I'm always loved pink.
The color of my childhood,
Tropical birds,
And other animals that are unique.
Shells that make you smile
And seafood that tastes good,
But sometimes smells vile."

"So is pink your favorite color?"
The friend asks. Then with a sarcastic frown,
"Please don't say your favorite is really brown!"
"No! Absolutely not," she says with a grin.
"But I'm not so sure,"
She says once again.

"I've always loved lavender.
It's elegant and pure;
The color of many things in nature.
Fruits, flowers, and even bugs.
And it smells like comforting hugs.
Even some rocks are colored lavender jade.
It's a truly unique shade."

"So, might lavender be your favorite color?"
The friend asks though she knows…
"I'm not so sure."
Says the girl with a mischievous smile,
"Sorry, but there's another color
That makes my days worthwhile."

"I've always loved the color green.

Its many shades and uses.
The color of the grass,
Of trees, and their beautiful leaves.
The color of nature as a whole.
Color of life and growth
One of the most beautiful
On earth."

"You sure can't choose a favorite color, can you?"
Asks her friend.
"I've tried many times,"
The girl says,
"But this is always how it will end.
I love every color
In God's book of creations.
It's all beautiful to me
To see the colors in His
Artistic illustrations."

"Expression"

A smile can show all of your joy
A little smirk to make you seem coy
A laugh to show you thought something was funny
A scrunch of the nose to look like a bunny
Tears in your eyes for pain, anger, or fear
Expressions for feelings you'll remember the next year

A slap in the face to show your disgust
A scream or a yell for things to be just
A hug from behind to show someone love
A hand intertwined in another's knitted glove
A kiss on the cheek that'll make you feel weak
A tiptoe around and you'll look like a sneak
A pat on the back to show congratulations
A wave to say hello or salutations

A painting to express your deepest emotion
A photo that gives one a specific notion
A drawing that shows a longing for the ocean
A poem to express every unsaid feeling
A verse about Christ's miraculous healing

So many ways to show expression
The most beautiful joy or darkest depression
Hints of God all over the Earth

Creativity has a very great worth
He is deep within the smallest details
Showing expression through even the smallest snails
Or through the largest of blue whales
His design is flawlessly stunning
Beauty flowing like rivers forever running

I love to see the expressions of His Creation
It's all across every tongue, tribe, and nation
The different ways we express ourselves
Is like 1,000 different stories found on bookshelves
I praise Him for the beauty of Expression
His stamp in every detailed impression

"Proud Of You"

Today I wore jeans that reminded me of you
Black mom jeans with rips in the knees
Like the ones you wear too
The problem with those jeans
Is they don't cover the scars you have

Fresh scab on your thigh
I caught a glimpse one night
It hurts to see you hurting
I wish your darkness would turn to light

I wish I could heal every wound
In your soul,
On your heart,
And skin.
I can't imagine the pain you carry
And the battles you face within.

I'm so proud for the fight you put up
And the strength you constantly show.
Even in the tears
You project strength beyond your years.
You have such pure beauty
In your amazing young soul
And the truth is that
Even in your pain
You really, truly glow.

"Maddie"

You're beautiful
You're lovely
On the outside
And within
I wish you could see a glimpse
Of what I see
When you grin

Your eyes light up with joy
And your smile brightens a room
Your laughter is so pretty
And your hair smells of sweet perfume
With compliments you shy away
And with your hair, you nervously play
Like it's in some nonexistent fray
Your hugs are some of the best
When I feel depressed

You're beautiful
You're lovely
In absolutely every way
I wish you could see the perfection
I see in you every day

"The Right Person"

You won't find the right person for you
Until you can be the right person yourself
Don't set standards you can't meet
Because if you can't equal those you set
The less than is all you can expect

"My Favorite"

You're one of my favorite chapters
One of my favorite pages
One I read over and over
Wishing we stayed in those stages
You're one of my favorite poems
Bitter and sweet
Painful yet beautiful
A written art form so short
Not lasting long, petite
But you're one of my favorite chapters
I will forever go back and reread
With a smile on my face
As my heart, again, will bleed

"Heart In The Mail"

My heart is in the mail.
I don't know when I'll get it back.
My heart is in the mail.
In a package that I can't track.
You took my heart 700 miles away
And told promises that you would stay,
But now my heart is in a box
Shipping back from more than just a few blocks.
I don't know when I will get it back,
But until then I'm on this painful track.
A train of new discovery
And heart surgery recovery.
But when it is returned
I'm sure much will have been learned
And life will again be lovely.
At least it is in 1 piece instead of 52.
It may not be in perfect condition,
But at least it's not broken, beaten, and bruised.
I don't know when I'll get it back,
But I know when I do
I won't look back and wish it had
Never been held by you.

"Horizon"

On the horizon I see a light
That breaks the darkness of night
Ships sail across the sea
And the ocean sings a song to me
Of crashing waves, breaking free

Creatures swim to and fro
And nature sings another song I wish to know
Of worship and praise to royalty
Creation obeying Him with glee
In the intricate storyline
That began with the light
That now shines so bright
And has broken the darkness of the night

"Long Distance Friends"

You live 10 hundred miles away
So far
But it feels like we've never been apart
You make me laugh but you never make me cry
Long distance best friend
You're my ride or die
Real test of friendship
Is one that's long distance
Miles apart but never left each other's side
That's a true friendship that will never die

"Scrapbook"

Paste in the pictures of days that passed
And write down the dates to match the scenes
Look at the pictures, smiling back
And remember how things used to be
Nothing better than blessings like that
Of joy and happy memories

"Grow"

Growing in different directions
And blooming in different sections
But my roots are all the same
My branches twist and turn like art
That no one could ever frame
And though they try to chop me down
They always fall and fail
And my fruit comes back in the next spring
Heavier on the scale
And so I continue to grow strong
As I sway within the breeze
And remember how He takes care
Of everyone of His beloved trees

The story of Him, the story of us.

The beginning.

Life out of dust
Breath of life in my lungs.
Created to create
Created out of His love.
My Father looked
At me and called me Good.
His creation,
Another beautiful thing,
Created in His image,
Marked by His love.
I am His daughter.
His heir. His son.
I am held by the perfect One.

The fall.

Temptation dangled in front of me
This looks really pretty!
Lies told by a friendly snake
"This is good and it's yours,
For you to take."
Slowly I begin

To feel the weight
Of my heart caving in
I want the thing he offers me,
Who cares if it's a sin!
Take a bite then plunge right in
Nakedness felt from within,
Hiding behind the leaves so thin,
But He can see behind it all
I can't hide behind a bush
Or even the tallest wall!
A chasm is formed
Between me and the One I once called "Lord"
I turn my back and remind myself that now I serve a different god
I'll take the path that is easy and broad

The birth.

In a world ravaged by sin
The people await a Savior.
On a silent night
So beautiful and quiet
A young virgin girl is visited
By an unexpected guest
An angel telling her that she will be greatly blessed

She's overwhelmed with emotion
Fear and anxiety trumped by her devotion
As she trusts God to do
Exactly what is best.

The Messiah long awaited
The King of the Jews
The one who will be called Savior
Born in a measly manger
A shift happens in the air
Because the earth knows
The Creator is here!
The shepherds watch and stare
In the silence of the night
They cry, "holy holy"
He's come to make it right!
Kings come seeking from afar
Following a bright, burning star
Looking for a king
But finding a child
Gifts for him they bring

The crucifixion.

I took the breath He gave me
And used it to speak against Him.

"Crucify Him!" I yelled
As He gazed upon my face
I ignored the look in His eyes
Screamed, "Kill Him!"
And profaned His name.
Days before I had praised Him,
Proclaimed, "Hosanna! God's Son!"
And laid my garment on the ground
Five days later I made a different sound
I spit and beat and mocked Him
But His love never changed.
I hung Him on that cross and still He pleaded my case?
The sinless died a sinners death, yet still I felt no shame
Because maybe He had loved me,
But I could easily forget His name.

Risen.

Jesus, a name I couldn't forget
It had been 3 days,
The day He claimed that He would raise.
His eyes began to haunt me,
That look I'd tried to ignore.
But that was before…

When He died, the rocks split,
The temple curtain tore
IN TWO!
The sky turned the darkest gray,
Yet it had just been a beautiful blue!
I couldn't forget all that had happened
How He still asked God to give me grace
And now I can't help but wonder,
Was He really taking my place?
And in the thoughtful stress and confusion
I hear someone whisper my name
With love and compassion and mercy
When it should be filled with blame
No one says my name the way He does
No one knows me like Him
I turned to see His beautiful face
And I race to hug Him with the biggest embrace
My sorrow turned into joy... and then right back around
"I spit at you and laughed at you
As they threw you to the ground!
I yelled for them to kill you
And with thorns you were crowned!
How do you say my name like that?
How come you don't accuse me?

How are you even here?
You were surely dead, how can this be?!"
He looked at me and smiled
And love reached His eyes
"I told you that I would die
And that again I would arise
And because I love you so
I forgive you for all you've done
I love you with an everlasting love
You're still my daughter
You're still my son!"

The Gift.

In the end, He still shocked me
He gave me something I do not deserve.
I **killed** Him and yet He still sought to serve
When He returned to Heaven,
He gave me the most incredible gift,
His presence in the Holy Spirit!
I nailed Him to that tree
And yet He says that *He* wants *me?!*

Who am I?

I am Rehab, grafted in

I am Gomer, chased down and redeemed
I am Gideon, used to lead
I am Moses, used to speak
I am David, crowned as royalty
I am Joseph, blessed after trial
I am Mary, given opportunity
I am Esther, favored by The King
I am Paul, hand picked
I am Barabas, with whom He traded places
I am Matthew, given grace
I am Peter, built upon
I am the woman breaking the perfume vase
I am a child of the Most High God
Called good,
And forgiven,
And loved.
The words of the devil are discredited
I am defined by The All Mighty One
He has given me a new name
A new description
I am not who the devil labeled me
I am someone new and free
Lies replaced with truth
By The One who died and rose again
I am covered by His grace,
And released of my sin!

"Who is He?" you may ask...
He. is the I Am.

Made in the USA
Coppell, TX
18 April 2024